D1263590

PRESIDENTS *and* FIRST LADIES

ABRAHAM & MARY TODD
LINCOLN

By

Ruth Ashby

WORLD ALMANAC® LIBRARY

Please visit our web site at: www.worldalmanaclibrary.com
For a free color catalog describing World Almanac® Library's list of high-quality books
and multimedia programs, call 1-800-848-2928 (USA) or 1-800-387-3178 (Canada).
World Almanac® Library's fax: (414) 332-3567.

Library of Congress Cataloging-in-Publication Data

Ashby, Ruth.
    Abraham & Mary Todd Lincoln / by Ruth Ashby.
      p. cm — (Presidents and first ladies)
    Includes bibliographical references and index.
    ISBN 0-8368-5695-3 (lib. bdg.)
    ISBN 0-8368-5701-1 (softcover)
    1. Lincoln, Abraham, 1809-1865—Juvenile literature. 2. Presidents—United States—Biography—
Juvenile literature. 3. Lincoln, Mary Todd, 1818-1882—Juvenile literature. 4. Presidents' spouses—
United States—Biography—Juvenile literature. 5. Lincoln, Abraham, 1809-1865—Marriage—
Juvenile literature. 6. Lincoln, Mary Todd, 1818-1882—Marriage—Juvenile literature. 7. Married
people—United States—Biography—Juvenile literature. I. Title.
E457.905.A83   2004
973.7'092'2—dc22
[B]   2004041950

First published in 2005 by
World Almanac® Library
330 West Olive Street, Suite 100
Milwaukee, WI 53132 USA

Copyright © 2005 by World Almanac® Library.

Produced by Byron Preiss Visual Publications Inc.
Project Editor: Kelly Smith
Photo Researcher: Larry Schwartz
Designed by Four Lakes Colorgraphics Inc.
World Almanac® Library editorial direction: Mark J. Sachner
World Almanac® Library editor: Jenette Donovan Guntly
World Almanac® Library art direction: Tammy West
World Almanac® Library graphic designer: Steve Schraenkler
World Almanac® Library production: Jessica Morris

Photo Credits: AP/Wide World: 12; The Chicago Historical Society: 5, 19; CORBIS: 11, 24 (bottom);
Illinois State Historical Society: 6, 16; HistoryPictures.com: 17; Keya Gallery: 18, 27; Library of Congress:
4 (top and bottom), 8 (bottom), 10, 13, 14, 23, 24 (top), 25, 26, 28, 31 (top and bottom), 32, 33, 34, 35, 37,
38 (top and bottom), 39, 40, 42; Courtesy of the Lincoln Museum, Fort Wayne, IN: 21, 29; Lincoln North:
The Joseph N. Nathanson Collection of Lincolniana. Rare Books and Special Collections Division McGill
Northern Illinois University: 8 (top); University Libraries, Montreal, Canada: 7; J. Vita: 22

Printed in the United States of America

1 2 3 4 5 6 7 8 9 08 07 06 05 04

CONTENTS

Words that appear in the glossary are printed in
boldface type the first time they occur in the text.

INTRODUCTION · · · · · ·

Abraham and Mary Todd Lincoln are one of the most memorable and, in some ways, controversial couples in American history. Much criticized in his lifetime, Abraham Lincoln is admired, even revered, today as the man who guided the nation through the fiery trial of the American Civil War and freed the slaves. His **assassination** in the wake of victory made him a legend. Mary Todd, however, has been judged more harshly. Though pitied as the wife of a slain president, she has also been criticized as a nagging wife, an extravagant first lady, and even, at the end of her life, a crazy widow.

Yet Mary was not as flawed, and Abraham was not as saintly, as legend would have it seem. They were both imperfect human beings challenged by extraordinary circumstances: the death of children, the disintegration of their country, and the threat of assassination. Through it all, they remained in love and committed to each other. Once, while watching Mary at a White House reception, Abraham Lincoln remarked that "my wife is as handsome as when she was a girl and I, a poor nobody then, fell in love with her and once more, have never fallen out." Mary, for her part, clung to Abraham as her "lover—husband—father—all."

Their lives, full of triumph and tragedy, began along the western frontier of a still-young country.

These companion photographs of Abraham and Mary Todd Lincoln were taken in 1846, when Abraham was thirty-seven and Mary twenty-eight years old. "They are very precious to me," Mary said later, "taken when we were young and so desperately in love."

WILDERNESS BOY

Lincoln the Rail-Splitter, painting by
J. L. G. Ferris, c. 1909.

Abraham Lincoln once wrote that his childhood could be summed up in a line from a well-known English poem: "The short and simple annals of the poor." No one watching him as a boy, dressed in buckskins and a coonskin cap and reading by the light of the hearth fire, could have imagined his remarkable future.

Lincoln came from a long line of pioneers, hardworking settlers who emigrated from England in 1637 and pushed westward into Massachusetts, Pennsylvania, and Virginia. In the early 1780s, his grandfather Abraham settled his family in the rich farmland of Kentucky. He was attacked by American Indians in his own cornfield, leaving his son Thomas an orphan at the age of six. Growing up "in poverty and in a new country," as Abraham later said of his father, Thomas "was left a wholly uneducated man."

However, Thomas was also a hard worker. By the time he was in his twenties, he had saved enough money to buy a farm and take a wife. Like her husband, dark-haired Nancy Hanks Lincoln was only semiliterate—able to read but barely able to write. The couple had a daughter, Sarah, and then a son: Abraham Lincoln was born on February 12, 1809, in a small log cabin, which was just sixteen by eighteen feet wide, with a dirt floor and no glass in the window. Abraham's cousin, Dennis Hanks, took one look and predicted that the bawling, red-faced infant would never amount to anything.

Abraham's first memories were of the farm on Knob Creek, where as a toddler he helped his father plant by dropping pumpkin seeds into the newly plowed earth. The family did not stay long in Kentucky, however. It was a slave state, and the Baptist church Tom and Nancy belonged to was against slavery. By the time Abraham was seven, Tom had decided to move his family to the brand-new state of Indiana, where slavery was outlawed. Abraham, big for his age, helped his father build a one-room cabin on the new homestead.

Within three years, Nancy had died and Tom Lincoln had gotten remarried to a warm and capable widow named Sarah Bush Johnston. She took the two Lincoln children under her wing, becoming, as Abraham remembered later, "a good and kind mother to me."

Sarah Lincoln, Abraham Lincoln's stepmother, in later years.

Between chores, Abraham and Sarah attended a neighborhood "blab school," a school in which children recited their lessons out loud. There Abraham learned "readin' and writin'." He practiced writing poetry in a copybook:

Abraham Lincoln is my name
And with my pen I wrote the same
I wrote in both haste and speed
And left it here for fools to read.

Educational opportunities were rare on the frontier, though. In total, Lincoln remembered, all his "schooling did not amount to one year."

Abraham was a serious student, eager to learn and to understand. "He must understand every thing—even to the smallest thing—minutely and exactly," Sarah Lincoln remembered later. "He would then repeat it over and over to himself again and again."

Reading was his great passion. "Abe was getting hungry for book[s]," Dennis Hanks remembered, "reading every thing he could lay his hands on." He would walk 20 miles (32 kilometers) to get a book he hadn't read. He especially loved history and biographies of the Founding Fathers, such as George Washington. His reading instilled in him a love of American liberty and **democracy**.

Teenage Years

Meanwhile, Abraham was shooting up, standing almost 6 feet 4 inches (193 centimeters) tall by the time he was seventeen. Most of his time was claimed by work around his father's farm: planting and hoeing and harvesting, milking cows, chopping wood, and splitting rails. He gained a reputation as an expert axman. "He can sink an ax deeper into wood than any man I ever saw," a neighbor marveled. Yet this bookish young man did not enjoy manual labor.

Nineteen-year-old Abraham steers a flatboat down to New Orleans in this painting by Louis Bonhajo.

Abraham scorned the unintellectual life of his father, whom he felt was chained to the land and the growing season.

So Abraham began to explore other possibilities. He hired himself out to local farmers, attending "house raisings, log rolling, corn shucking and workings of all kinds," as an acquaintance remembered. He built a little flatboat and ferried passengers to steamboats going up and down the Ohio River. With a friend, he brought a flatboat loaded with fruits and vegetables down the Mississippi to the bustling port of New Orleans. It was Abraham's first visit to a big city, his first opportunity to mix with people from all over the world—British, Mexican, French, Spanish. It was also his first experience of slave auctions.

When he returned home, Abraham turned his earnings over to his father, as he always had, yet now he was practically twenty-one—almost old enough to vote and make his own way in the world. When Thomas decided to move the family once again, this time to Illinois, Abraham dutifully led a wagon team to the new homestead and helped clear the land. Then he took off, "a friendless, uneducated, penniless boy," he later wrote, who had finally "separated from his father."

This photograph of one of Lincoln's homes in New Salem, Illinois, was taken in the late nineteenth century. The cabin was typical of the rough-hewn structures built on the frontier.

Again he took a flatboat down to New Orleans, running aground on a **milldam** at a little Illinois town called New Salem. Townspeople watched, amused, as the young giant bored a hole in the bow so that the water ran out and the flatboat floated up and over the dam. Marveling at his ingenuity, a local businessman hired him to manage a general store in town. In July 1831, Lincoln came to New Salem to stay.

New Start in New Salem

The rough frontier town would be Lincoln's home for the next six years. He arrived as a "piece of floating driftwood," in his own words, and left as a lawyer and an elected state **legislator**. In between, he worked as a store manager, a land surveyor, a postmaster, a soldier, a carpenter, and a politician—anything that would enable him to earn a living. He soon became known for his friendliness and fund of humorous stories. Like his father, Abraham spun a good yarn and could keep his listeners entertained for hours. He was also admired for his strength. When the local gang of toughs challenged him to a fight, he wrestled the champion to a draw and earned the admiration of the crowd.

This print shows Abraham Lincoln as a clean-shaven lawyer in Springfield, Illinois. Within ten years of leaving New Salem, he would be one of the most successful lawyers in the state.

He was so popular that some of his friends suggested he go into politics. Lincoln seized the opportunity, declaring himself a candidate for the Illinois legislature in 1832. In his political platform, he declared that his ambition was "that of being truly esteemed of my fellow men, by rendering myself worthy of their esteem." He was distracted from campaigning when a conflict with Native Americans called the Black Hawk War broke out that summer. He spent a few months as captain of a volunteer **militia** but saw no action, only a "good many battles with mosquitoes." This was the only military service Lincoln would ever see. That fall, he went back to New Salem to be defeated in his first election.

The next few years were difficult. Lincoln invested in a store with another young man who died and left him with what he called "the National Debt." It would take Lincoln fifteen years to pay off the debt. In 1834, he ran for office again, and this time he won. At age twenty-five, Abraham took his seat in the Illinois legislature, where he fought for roads, canals, and banks for the growing state.

In his spare time, he began to study law. His New Salem neighbors grew accustomed to seeing him studying in the open air, stretched out on the ground with his feet propped up on a nearby tree. Once a fellow passed him sitting on a woodpile. "What are you reading?" asked the man. "I ain't reading; I'm studying law," Lincoln replied. "Good God Almighty!" the man exclaimed.

After three years of study, Abraham passed his law exam and was hired by a firm in Springfield, the new capital of Illinois. In April 1837, Lincoln packed his bags, borrowed a horse, stuck seven dollars in his pocket, and rode into Springfield to meet his future.

Slave vs. Free States

In the early 1800s, the United States maintained a fragile balance between slave states, where slavery was legal, and free states, where it was not. As the number of states increased, the balance was threatened. One visitor noted, "Old America seems to be breaking up and moving westward." Settlers from "old" states such as Pennsylvania and Virginia were loading up their wagons and pushing into land west of the Appalachian Mountains. New states were born every few years: Kentucky (1792), Tennessee (1796), Ohio (1803), Louisiana (1812), Indiana (1816), Mississippi (1817), Illinois (1818), and Alabama (1819). Each state had to make the momentous decision about slavery when it applied to enter the United States.

By 1819, there were eleven slave states and eleven free states. Then Missouri applied for statehood as a slave state and upset the balance of power. Northerners were alarmed. Kentucky **senator** Henry Clay, a friend of Mary Todd's family, proposed the Missouri Compromise, a plan to keep the number of slave and free states equal. It said that Missouri would be admitted as a slave state and Maine would be admitted as a free state. An imaginary line drawn at **latitude** 36° 30' N would be set as the permanent boundary between slave states in the South and free states in the North. The Missouri Compromise would stand until 1854.

CHAPTER TWO

KENTUCKY BELLE

The girl who would marry Abraham Lincoln grew up in a privileged world far from the poverty of the backwoods frontier. Mary Todd experienced comfort and elegance that the young Lincoln never knew. The Todd family home in Lexington, Kentucky, was an elegant brick building with nine rooms, a greenhouse, and a large garden. Mary's father, Robert Todd, was a banker, manufacturer, politician, and prominent citizen. Both of her grandfathers were founders of the town. Like her brothers and sisters, Mary was taught to be proud of her family heritage.

When Mary was born, on December 13, 1818, she was placed in the care of Mammy Sally, the slave woman who helped raise her. Mary's mother, Eliza, already had three older children and would give birth again a year later. She depended on slaves to help run her household, and Mary grew up accepting slavery as a part of life.

Slaves in the Todd family were kindly treated, and both of Mary's maternal grandmothers **emancipated** their slaves in their wills. However, Mary knew all about the darker side of slavery, too. On her way to school, she passed a whipping post where slaves were routinely beaten, and the wretched slave jail was just three blocks from her home. When Mammy Sally offered food and comfort to runaway slaves who knocked at the Todd's back door late at night, Mary sympathized and said not a word.

In this early photograph of Mary Todd Lincoln, taken when she was twenty-eight years old, Mary displays her fondness for patterned dresses. She especially liked stripes.

Motherless Girl

Mary's mother died of childbirth fever when Mary was only six. It was the first of many losses to devastate Mary in the course of her life. Her father promptly married again. Mary's stepmother, Betsy Humphreys Todd, was a stern, unsympathetic woman with high standards of dress and manners. "It takes six generations to make a lady," she was fond of reminding her stepchildren. None of the Todds qualified, and they all resented and disliked the new Mrs. Todd.

Temperamental Mary often fought with Betsy, and one of their first arguments was about clothes. Even at age nine, Mary was already keenly interested in fashion and fascinated by the wide hoops stylish women wore under their dresses. One morning, before church, she and a young relative fashioned homemade hoops out of willow reeds and stuck them under their skirts. "What frights you are," Mrs. Todd barked when she caught sight of them. "Take those awful things off, dress yourself properly, and go to Sunday school." Mary cried and never forgot the humiliation.

Yet there were happy times, too. Unlike many nineteenth-century fathers, Robert Todd believed in providing a good education for his daughters as well as for his sons. In 1827, when she was eight, Mary began to attend Ward's Female Academy, three blocks from home. There she learned reading, writing, and arithmetic, in addition to subjects such as geography, history, the natural sciences, French, and religion. She

Fashionable Bird Cages

The hoop skirts that Mary Todd craved at age nine became wider and wider as the century progressed. By midcentury, fashionable women wore circular steel hoops that looked like birdcages underneath their dresses. As much as 13 yards (12 meters) of fabric around at the base, gowns were decorated with an array of ribbons, lace, braids, and bows. In order to reduce their waists to the desired 18 inches (46 cm), women laced themselves into stiff whalebone **corsets**. Mary Todd tried to downplay her natural plumpness by lacing as tightly as possible. During the Civil War, when dresses were at their widest and gaudiest, Mary Todd Lincoln's were the most extravagant of all.

Well-dressed women like Mary Todd wore wire frames to puff out their skirts.

Mary Todd Lincoln in middle age, wearing a seed pearl necklace.

was an attentive and very successful student. A classmate remembered that Mary was "far in advance over other girls in education; she had a retentive memory and mind that enabled her to grasp and understand thoroughly that lesson she was required to learn."

She completed her education in the social graces at another local school, Madame Mentelle's. Eligible young women were expected to be an ornament to society, and it was here that Mary polished her skills in dancing, flower arranging, French, and polite conversation and etiquette. When her class put on a French play, attention-seeking Mary shone as the star.

Growing Up

By the time she was fourteen, Mary was ready to be launched into the social whirl of dances, tea parties, and late-night suppers. She was, as a friend described her, pretty and plump, with "clear blue eyes, long lashes, light brown hair with a glint of bronze, and a lovely complexion." Despite all her attractions, Mary did not have one special beau. Maybe it was because she was too outspoken and opinionated for most Lexington males. Mary had a gift for mimicking others and a sharp tongue she did not hesitate to use. Perhaps it was because she had a restless yearning for adventure.

In 1837, Mary visited two of her sisters in Springfield, Illinois. Her eldest sister, Elizabeth, had moved to Springfield after marrying Ninian Edwards, the son of a former Illinois governor. The next oldest sister, Frances, soon followed Elizabeth west. Mary found the young town exhilarating, a refreshing change from the stuffy parlors of Lexington. Not only that, it boasted two men to every woman.

Two years later, Elizabeth Edwards invited Mary to "make our home her home." Mary left her stepmother and her nine half sisters and half brothers behind and traveled by train, steamboat, and stagecoach to reach Springfield—and to find her destiny.

"LOVE IS ETERNAL"

Springfield in 1839 was still a raw prairie town with no sidewalks or street lamps. The unpaved streets were so muddy that one day after a rain, Mary Todd and a friend went out with their arms full of wooden shingles, which they threw down in front of them to keep their skirts clean.

As the new state capital, however, Springfield was a center of political power and was filled with young men hoping to make their mark on the world. The Edwards home attracted a group of sociable young people. Mary, eager for popularity, impressed other young women with her fluency in French and her flair for style. Flitting from picnic to dance to tea party, she was, an acquaintance remembered, the "very creature of excitement, and never enjoyed herself more than when in society and surrounded by a company of merry friends." Soon she had suitors: Edwin Webb, a lawyer and

The Illinois statehouse in Springfield, where Lincoln served in the legislature.

Stephen Douglas, known as the "Little Giant," was Mary Todd's beau, and, later, Abraham Lincoln's rival in Illinois politics.

legislator who was fifteen years older than she; and Stephen Douglas, a 5-foot-4-inch (163 cm) tall lawyer with a keen intellect and fierce ambition. Mary, however, was not looking for a man of wealth or family connections. She craved a union of heart and mind. To her sister she confided her idea of a perfect husband: "A good man, with a head for position, fame, and power, a man of mind with a hope and bright prospects rather than all the houses and gold in the world."

The man who would meet her criteria was also looking for a mate. Lincoln was thirty and eager to settle down, yet his social life was not a success. "I am quite as lonesome here as I ever was anywhere in my life," he confided to a friend. At 6 feet 4 inches (193 cm) tall, with a long, scraggly neck, unruly hair, and ill-fitting clothes, he looked as awkward in polite society as he felt. Mary's sister, Frances, called him "the plainest man in Springfield." Yet those who at first found him ugly often revised their opinion when they heard him speak.

A Different Courtship

Abraham Lincoln first espied Mary Todd, dressed in pink organdy fabric and lace, across a ballroom in December 1839. He moved across the room and confessed that he wanted to dance with her in the worst way. Later Mary would joke that he did indeed dance "in the worst way." Yet Mary soon discovered that beneath Abraham's rough exterior lay a keen mind, sharp wit, and gentle manner. These two highly intelligent people found that they could discuss politics, poetry, history, and literature. Soon Abraham was a frequent caller at the Edwards home. Mary confided to a friend that he had "the most congenial mind she had ever met." According to her niece, Abraham in turn found Mary a girl of great fun and bubbling enthusiasm who shared his passion for politics.

Sometime in December 1840, they probably became engaged, but both hesitated before making a full commitment. Many of their acquaintances thought the match unsuitable. Elizabeth Edwards warned Mary that "they were so different that they could not live happily as man and wife." Abraham was hurt by Elizabeth's obvious disapproval. "One *d* is enough for God," he said bitterly to a friend. "But the Todds need two."

Little had changed by late December, when Abraham promised to escort Mary to a party. He was late, and she left without him. When he arrived, he saw her flirting with Edwin Webb. According to Mary's sister, Lincoln appeared "grim and determined." When at last alone with Mary, he broke off the engagement. Hot-tempered Mary stamped her foot. "Go," she retorted, "and never come back."

Lincoln was devastated. Sunk into a deep depression, he took to his bed and missed a week in the legislature. Acquaintances whispered that he was having "two catfits and a duckfit." In keeping with traditions of that time, his roommate, Joshua Speed, removed Lincoln's razor from his room for fear he might hurt himself. "I am now the most miserable man living," Abraham wrote to his law partner, John Todd Stuart, a cousin of Mary Todd. "If what I feel were equally distributed to the whole human family, there would not be one cheerful face on [E]arth."

Mary also ached. Six months after the split, she wrote to a friend that Abraham "deems me unworthy of notice, as I have not met him in the gay world for months . . . yet I would the case were different . . . much happiness would it afford me."

The Ties That Bind

Mary Todd was giving up more than her single status when she married Abraham Lincoln. She also lost all her civil and legal rights. As noted English legal expert William Blackstone stated, "When a couple marries, they become one and the one is he."

For women of that time, marrying badly could be a lasting mistake. Even if Abraham had been a drunkard or a wife beater, Mary could not have left him. Legally, she belonged to him. Divorce laws were not liberalized until the end of the nineteenth century.

Mary did not need to worry about her husband, who treated women with care and respect. "Whatever woman may cast her lot with mine," Abraham wrote before he was married, "it is my intention to do all in my power to make her happy and contented." In his union with Mary Todd, he did his best to live up to his promise.

The marriage certificate of Abraham Lincoln and Mary Todd. They were married on Friday evening, November 4, 1842, in the presence of about thirty friends and relatives.

Wedding Party

It was not until the summer of 1842, more than a year later, that friends brought the two together again. Abraham and Mary began to meet secretly, and they came to an understanding. It was time to get married. Lincoln got a marriage license from the county court and ordered a wedding band.

At the last possible moment, Mary told Ninian and Elizabeth Edwards about her plans. When they saw they could not change her mind, they insisted that the ceremony be held in their home. Elizabeth quickly sent out wedding invitations and baked a wedding cake.

The following evening, November 4, about thirty guests gathered in the Edwardses' parlor for the ceremony. Mary wore her sister Frances's white satin dress and a pearl necklace. Abraham, dressed in a black suit, gave her a gold wedding band inscribed with the words *Love Is Eternal*.

On November 11, he wrote an acquaintance that there was "nothing new here, except my marrying, which to me, is a matter of profound wonder."

THE SPRINGFIELD YEARS

The marriage on which Abraham and Mary Todd Lincoln had embarked was in many ways a union of opposites. He was tall, she was short; he was thin, she was plump. She was a creature of nervous energy, excitable when happy and hysterical when upset. Abraham, in contrast, lapsed into periods of quiet despondency. Yet "notwithstanding our opposite natures," as Mary once said, "our lives have been eminently peaceful."

The newlyweds made their first home in a boardinghouse called the Globe Tavern, where for four dollars per week they received an 8-by-14-foot (2-by-4-meter) bedchamber and meals in the common dining room. It was the smallest place Mary had ever lived, but she did not complain. She was in love.

A view of downtown Springfield. Lincoln's law office with his partner, William Herndon, was in the second-to-the-last building on the right. By 1869, when this photograph was taken, the streets had been lined with wooden sidewalks.

A recently discovered photograph of a little boy possibly identified as Edward Baker Lincoln, the second son of Abraham and Mary Todd Lincoln.

Soon Mary had an all-consuming interest. Nine months after her wedding, she gave birth to a son, whom she named Robert Todd after her father. After the birth, Mary awoke to see her "darling husband, . . . bending over me, with such love and tenderness." Until now, Abraham had called his wife "Molly," or sometimes "little woman," or "child-wife." Now he often called her "Mother." Mary was as contented as she would ever be. "I believe a nice home, a loving husband, and precious child are the happiest stages of life," she wrote to her daughter-in-law years later.

Lincoln energetically set to work to provide for his family. His final term as state legislator had ended in March 1842, after which he became a full-time lawyer with a busy practice. Much of his time was spent riding a circuit, trying cases in courtrooms throughout the state. He spent six months each year on the road, leaving Mary to run the household alone.

Family Circle

By 1844, Abraham had earned enough money to put down $1,200 on a house on the corner of Eighth and Jackson Streets. It was small, just a story and a half, but it had a real back yard for Bobby, and, later, little Eddie, who was born in 1846.

By then, Abraham was making enough money for Mary to hire a servant, but most of the time, she did all the work herself, baking, cooking, cleaning, and sewing. When he was home, Abraham helped her out by grocery shopping and watching the children. The Lincolns were doting parents. Lincoln pulled his boys in carts and took them to the office, where they exasperated his law partner, William Herndon, who called them "brats." Herndon wanted to "wring their necks and throw them out the window," but Lincoln, he said, "worshipped his children."

Mary, too, adored her "angel boys" and was an affectionate mother. She was also anxious and easily panicked. Once, when Bobby swallowed some strong chemicals used to keep the outhouse clean, she dashed out into the street screaming, "Bobby will die! Bobby will die!" Abraham had to rush home from work to assure her that Bobby would be all right.

When Mary suffered from migraines and took to her bed, Abraham watched the boys. When she had a tantrum, he got out of the way. Mary had always been subject to mood swings. Before her marriage, she was, as her cousin said, "very highly strung, nervous, impulsive, irritable, having an emotional temperament much like an April day, running all over with laughter one moment, at the next

Lincoln's law office in Springfield. It was usually very messy, littered with piles of books and documents. Lincoln relied on his very good memory to keep his business in order.

crying as though her heart would break." Now, as she juggled the demands of housekeeping, children, and a husband, the stress sometimes overwhelmed her.

Lincoln himself could be a trial. He was moody, too, often absentminded or withdrawn into silence. His frontier informality could drive Mary crazy. No matter how much care she took with his appearance, he often looked disheveled, and he had a distressing way of answering the door in his shirtsleeves. Sometimes Mary would find him stretched out across the hallway floor reading a book.

Getting into Politics

Mary was not worried merely about what the neighbors would think. She was trying to groom her husband for life in the public eye. Both Lincolns had strong political ambitions, and in these early years, Mary took an active role in promoting his career. In 1846, when Abraham became a candidate for **Congress**, Mary surprised her neighbors with her knowledge of politics. When he won the seat, she was thrilled.

After the election, a Virginian visiting Springfield remarked on Abraham's popularity in Illinois. "Yes," Mary replied, "he is a great favorite everywhere. He is to be President of the United States some day; if I had not thought so I never would have married him, for you can see he is not pretty. But look at him! Doesn't he look as if he would make a magnificent president?" It was not the last time Mary would predict that Abraham was destined for the presidency.

However, Lincoln's two years in the **House of Representatives** were a disappointment to both of them. Ignored by Washington society, Mary became bored and soon retreated with the children back to her father's home in Lexington. Abraham did not make much of an impression in Congress and was not **renominated** by the **Whig Party**. When his term was up, the whole family went back to Springfield and settled in for the next ten years.

On February 1, 1850, the couple suffered a piercing loss when their younger son, Eddie, died of **tuberculosis**. Both parents were devastated. However, Abraham, saying only that "we miss him very much," was able to take refuge in his work. For Mary, who lived for her children, the pain was nearly unbearable. Concerned for her health, Abraham urged her to recover. "Eat, Mary, for we must live," he reminded her. The death of children was common in the nineteenth century, and good Christians were expected to accept suffering as the will of God, yet Mary could not find consolation in religion. Years later, she wrote to a friend, "I grieve to say that even at this distant day, I do not feel sufficiently submissive to our loss."

Three weeks later, Mary found she was pregnant, and on December 21, 1850, little William Wallace Lincoln was born. Eager for a girl, they tried again, but on April 4, 1853, they had yet another boy, whom they named Thomas, after Abraham's father. Soon the baby's large head and wiggly body earned him the nickname "Tadpole," or "Tad."

After his return from Washington, Lincoln resumed his lucrative law practice. He made enough for Mary to enlarge the house and buy expensive new furnishings. He was still hungry for political office, however. It was a hunger encouraged by Mary. William Herndon, Lincoln's law partner, wrote that Mary was "like a toothache, keeping her husband awake to politics day and night." When Abraham once complained, "Nobody knows me," Mary replied prophetically, "They will."

Antislavery Spokesman

It was a stormy time to be in politics. In the 1850s, the issue of slavery was dividing America. Lincoln had hated slavery since the time he was a boy, but he was no **abolitionist**. He reasoned that because slavery was legal under the United States Constitution, it could not be outlawed in states in which it already existed. The main challenge for him, as for others who were not strongly for or against abolition, was to keep slavery from expanding—especially into the new territories.

Tad Lincoln, dressed in the uniform of a **Union** colonel, about 1864.

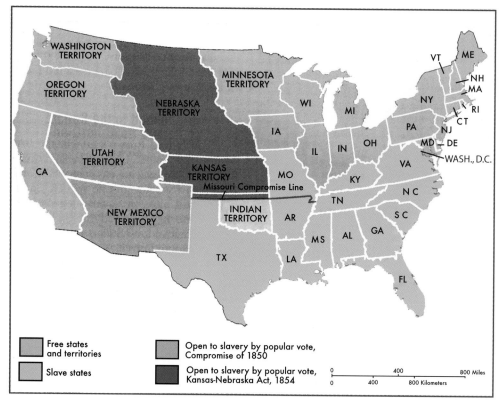

Slavery in the United States, 1854. In the course of the early and middle nineteenth century, the U.S. Congress passed a series of compromises to decide slavery in the territories and new states: The Missouri Compromise (1820), the Compromise of 1850, and the Kansas-Nebraska Act (1854).

He was alarmed at a new measure that might extend the reach of slavery. Mary's old beau, Stephen Douglas, now a senator from Illinois, introduced a bill proposing that the Nebraska Territory be divided into two parts, Kansas and Nebraska. In each, settlers would be able to vote on whether the territory would allow slavery or not. The Kansas-Nebraska Act, as Douglas's bill was called, contradicted the Missouri Compromise of 1820, which explicitly forbade slavery so far north. Nonetheless, Southern congressmen were in favor of it.

Congress passed the Kansas-Nebraska Act in 1854. In reaction, Lincoln decided to join the new Republican Party, which was dedicated to halting the expansion of slavery. He also decided to run for the Senate. He had already been denied the nomination once by the Whigs. This time, he would be running as a Republican against the Democratic nominee, Stephen Douglas. At the Republican State Convention, Lincoln delivered a speech that would make him famous across the nation: "A house divided against itself cannot stand. I believe this government cannot endure, permanently half slave and half free."

All that long, hot summer of 1858, Abraham crisscrossed Illinois, attending rallies and debating Douglas. Mary stayed home with the boys, attending only the last of the seven debates. However, she campaigned, too, among Springfield friends and neighbors. "Mr. Douglas is a very little, little giant by the side of my tall Kentuckian," she would boast.

When the votes were counted, Douglas won the Senate race. The Lincolns were disappointed but not despondent. "I feel like the boy who stumped his toe," Abraham said. "I am too big to cry and too badly hurt to laugh." In any event, the debates made his reputation.

"We Are Elected!"

Two years later, when the Republicans began to look for a presidential candidate, Lincoln's name was on everyone's lips. Still, it was a surprise when he was nominated at the Republican National

This campaign portrait of presidential candidate Abraham Lincoln is based on an 1859 photograph. After the election, an eleven-year-old girl named Grace Bedell wrote him a letter suggesting he grow a beard because his face was too thin. Lincoln decided to take her advice.

The Prairies Are on Fire

The Lincoln-Douglas debates electrified the nation in the summer of 1858. "The prairies are on fire," one New York reporter wrote. In seven three-hour debates, the Little Giant and Long Abe kept their audiences riveted. In a booming voice, the 5-foot-4-inch (163 cm) Douglas defended the doctrine of popular sovereignty—the idea that people themselves should be able to decide whether to permit slavery in the territories where they lived. Lincoln retorted, "If slavery is not wrong, nothing is wrong." Slavery, he insisted, was a great evil that should be kept out of the territories. Not only that, he went on, but "there is no reason in the world why the Negro is not entitled to all the natural rights enumerated in the Declaration of Independence, the right to life, liberty, and the pursuit of happiness. I hold that he is as much entitled to these as the white man."

By the time the debates were over, Lincoln had the attention of the nation.

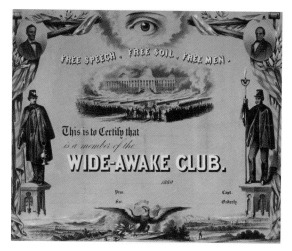

A membership certificate for the Wide-Awake Club, a popular Republican marching club. Throughout Lincoln's campaign, young men, dressed in short capes and caps, marched in torchlight processions, holding banners that read "The Great Rail-splitter." In the upper corners are medallions of Lincoln (left) and **running mate** Hannibal Hamlin (right).

Convention in May 1860. In those days, presidential candidates let their supporters do their campaigning for them, so the Lincolns stayed home in Springfield that summer. Politicians and reporters flocked to the town to size them up. Mary was gratified when the *New York Tribune* called her "amiable and accomplished . . . vivacious and graceful . . . a sparkling talker."

On election day, November 6, 1860, Lincoln remained in the Springfield telegraph office long enough to be sure that he had really won. Then he slipped out to tell his wife.

"Mary, Mary, we are elected!"

The 1860 Republican National Convention was held in the "Wigwam," a public hall in Chicago. Abraham Lincoln won the nomination for president on the third ballot.

CHAPTER FIVE

THE PRESIDENT AND MRS. LINCOLN

"Well, boys," Lincoln told a group of reporters the day after the election, "your troubles are over now, mine have just begun." The president-elect faced a daunting challenge. Although he had repeatedly assured the Southern states that he would not interfere with slavery there, they did not believe him. One by one, they began to **secede** from the United States—first South Carolina in December 1860, then six others. The rebellious states formed a new nation, the **Confederate States of America**. Lame-duck James Buchanan (the president leaving office) sat back and did nothing. Lincoln would have to deal with the mounting conflict.

When Abraham Lincoln took office, the nation faced the worst crisis since the Revolutionary War. The Civil War erupted little more than a month after his **inauguration**.

Mary, however, was in a flurry of excitement: her lifelong dream had come true. In January, she took a shopping trip to New York to prepare for her new role as first lady. Already she had heard rumors that her taste in clothing was unsophisticated and unfashionably western. She was determined to prove her critics wrong.

Even Mary could not ignore the hate mail that poured into the house, though. One letter included a sketch of Abraham tarred and feathered, with a noose around his neck. Another showed the devil pitching Lincoln into the fires of hell. Even more disturbing were Lincoln's premonitions of death. One day, as he rested on the sofa in

Fashionable ladies show off their finery at the Lincoln inaugural ball, March 4, 1865, in this illustration from a popular magazine. Mary Todd Lincoln enjoyed herself at the ball and was praised for her performance. "She is more self-possessed than her husband," decided the *New York Herald*.

his bedroom, he saw a double reflection of his face in the opposite mirror. One image was "flushed with life," the other "deathly pale." When he asked Mary for an interpretation, she told him it meant that he would live in his first term as president but die in his second. Shaken, they both tried to dismiss the vision from their minds.

On February 11, 1861, Lincoln and his family boarded a train for Washington. Less than a month later, he delivered his **inaugural address**. He promised the South there would be no war unless they started it and appealed to their common heritage as Americans. We "must not break our bonds of affection," he said.

His appeal was in vain. On April 12, Confederate guns opened fire on Fort Sumter, the federal fort in the harbor of Charleston, South Carolina. These were the first shots fired in the Civil War. Four more states quickly joined the Confederacy.

Lincoln immediately called up the federal troops. A week later, Washington was overrun by soldiers who poured in from all over the North. They pitched tents in the park south of the White House and built **barracks**, barricades, and hospitals. Their presence further cluttered the already dirty, unfinished city.

Living in the White House

The White House itself, as one of Mary's cousins sniffed, was "seedy and dilapidated." When Mary moved in, she was delighted to learn that Congress had allotted $20,000 for redecoration. She set about transforming the old thirty-one-room house into a refined and elegant residence fit for a president. She purchased new White House china, emblazoned with the coat of arms of the United States. She bought gold-fringed draperies for the Green Room and velvet wallpaper for the East Room.

Mrs. Lincoln with two of her sons, Willie (left) and Tad (right).

Soon the White House was presentable, even handsome. However, as usual, Mary had overspent her allowance. Abraham, annoyed, said he would pay for what she had overspent out of his own pocket. The resourceful Mary found other ways to pay the bills.

Life in the White House quickly settled into a routine. Lincoln breakfasted early on coffee, eggs, and toast and went over his mail with his private secretary, John Hay. Meetings and visits began at ten o'clock in the morning. Every day at four o'clock, Mary insisted that Abraham go out for a drive. She was very concerned for her overworked husband, and made sure that he remembered to eat and got enough rest and relaxation. It was his job to take care of the country; she took care of him.

On Friday nights, Abraham would hold levees, or open receptions, for whoever stopped by. Lincoln called them his "public opinion baths." When not crippled by one of her blinding headaches, Mary would go, too. On Saturday afternoons, people would arrive by invitation only.

Mary Lincoln, dressed in one of her elegant gowns.

Despite the pressures of the war, the Lincolns' first year in the White House had its happy moments. Their two younger sons were growing up. In many ways like his father, Willie was a gentle, good-natured child, eager for knowledge and interested in books. He loved the railroad and memorized timetables and railroad stations. Tad, who had difficulty learning to read and speak, probably had what today we would call a learning disability. Warmhearted and irrepressible, he was his father's favorite.

Together with their menagerie of rabbits, kittens, ponies, and even goats, the boys kept the White House lively. One group of tourists found Tad in the East Room "cracking a whip" over two goats "hitched" to a chair. Some staff members called Willie and Tad spoiled and undisciplined, especially when Tad shot into the room during a cabinet meeting and plopped on his father's lap.

Lincoln, though, was uncritical of his "two little codgers." Playing with his sons allowed him to escape from the pressures of the war. He wrestled with them on Mary's new carpets and brought them with him when he reviewed the troops. Years after he had died, Mary recalled Abraham saying, "It is my pleasure that my children are free and happy, and unrestrained by parental tyranny. Love is the chain whereby to bind a child to its parents."

Mary indulged in her favorite extravagance, clothes. For the first time in her life, she had her own private dressmaker, a former slave named Elizabeth Keckley, with whom she became good friends. The first lady kept Keckley busy making the latest French fashions. Mary favored bright colors, such as white, blue, yellow, and purple, low-cut dresses, and fresh flowers in her hair. The effect was luxurious and sometimes overwhelming. After attending an East Room reception, a senator from Oregon complained that Mrs. Lincoln had "her bosom on exhibition and a flower pot on her head, while there was a train of silk or satin, dragging on the floor behind her." Mary didn't care. To those who thought she was overdressed, she snapped, "I want the women to mind their own business. I intend to wear what I please."

Elizabeth Keckley was First Lady Mary Lincoln's best friend and confidante. After Abraham Lincoln's assassination, Keckley wrote a memoir of her days in the White House, and Mary refused ever to speak to her again.

A Sudden Tragedy

Early in 1862, Mary Lincoln decided to give a party that she hoped would establish her as Washington's leading hostess. For the occasion, she chose a ruffled white satin gown adorned with flowers and wore a wreath of flowers in her hair. The evening was a brilliant

In the Public Eye

Both Lincolns were attacked repeatedly by the press during their lifetimes. Abraham was called a "backwoods president," a "tyrant," and a "gorilla." People criticized Lincoln's manners, his accent, his clothes, and his handling of the war.

Yet Mary, who wanted deeply to be popular, seemed singled out for special and unceasing criticism. She was criticized for buying velvet and silk and holding extravagant parties when soldiers were dying. Worst of all, she was blamed by the Northern press for being a Southerner and was even suspected of being a spy. Mary could not understand such accusations. "Why should I sympathize with the rebels?" she asked. "Are they not against me? They would hang my husband tomorrow if it was in their power."

To make matters worse, the Southern press—and even some members of her own family—charged her with being a traitor. Three of her Confederate half brothers and one brother-in-law died during the war. Mary grieved their loss, but in private. "I seem to be a scapegoat for both North and South!" she concluded in despair.

success. The *Washington Star* said that it was "the most superb affair of its kind ever seen here."

No one watching Mary greeting her guests that night would have guessed she was in a state of extreme anxiety. Upstairs, eleven-year-old Willie lay sick with **typhoid fever** brought on by contaminated water. All night, the worried parents took turns running upstairs and tending to their son.

Willie kept getting worse, and two weeks later, he was dead. Abraham was devastated. "It is hard, hard, to have him die," he confessed. Once a week, for months afterward, he would lock himself in the room where Willie had died and grieve alone. Mary, though, gave way to complete despair. She took to her bed, weeping and calling out to Willie. Lincoln was so concerned for her mental health that one day he led her to a window and pointed to a mental hospital in the distance. "Try and control your grief," he said, "or it will drive you mad, and we may have to send you there."

Gradually the sobbing subsided, and Mary again took up the burden of daily life, yet she was never able to accept Willie's death. Five months later, she wondered if "our heavenly father has forsaken us in removing so lovely a boy from us."

All across America, other mothers and fathers grieved, too, for sons fallen in battle. The war that many had thought would be over in three months was now in its second year. And there was no end in sight.

CHAPTER SIX

WHEN THIS CRUEL WAR IS OVER

President Lincoln's war was not going well. By 1862, the Civil War had settled into a numbingly destructive pattern in which both sides lost enormous numbers of men, but neither gained a decisive advantage. In the East, where the federal goal was to capture the Confederate capital of Richmond, Virginia, Union troops had yet to win a battle. The brilliant tactics of Confederate general Robert E. Lee successfully kept them from approaching the capital. This series of defeats was demoralizing for ordinary soldiers and their commander in chief alike. "We are whipped again," Lincoln moaned when he received news of yet another Union disaster.

Confederate general Robert E. Lee, the brilliant commander of the Army of Northern Virginia.

Only in the West, where Union general Ulysses S. Grant won victories at Fort Donelson and Shiloh, did federal troops seem to be making any progress. On April 25, Union Flag Officer David Glasgow Farragut took the crucial city of New Orleans. River by river and fort by fort, the North slowly captured the major trade and communication routes that fed the South.

General Ulysses S. Grant, Lincoln's favorite Union general. After Grant's many victories in the West, Lincoln brought him East in February 1864 to fight General Robert E. Lee in Virginia.

A group of former slaves, or contrabands, dressed in old Union uniforms. Before the **Emancipation Proclamation**, most Union officers refused to return escaped slaves to their former owners, declaring that they were property of war, or "**contraband**." Even after emancipation, the name stuck.

Meanwhile, both sides were suffering heavy losses. In the two days of fighting at Shiloh in Tennessee, on April 6–7, 1862, Union **casualties** totaled 13,000 dead, wounded, or missing, and Confederate casualties totaled 9,500. "Men were lying in every conceivable position," a soldier from Tennessee remembered later, "the dead lying with their eyes wide open, the wounded begging piteously for help."

In fact, Shiloh was the bloodiest battle ever fought in North America up to that time. It was just the beginning. As battle followed battle and casualty lists were posted in every village, town, and city across the North and the South, the whole nation went into shock.

Lending a Helping Hand

During the summer of 1862, Mary Lincoln found some comfort in visiting Washington hospitals where other women's sons lay wounded. She brought the soldiers flowers and fruit and sat at their bedsides reading books and writing letters. "Among the many ladies who visit the hospitals none is more indefatigable than Mrs. Lincoln," one newspaper reported.

Mary also became more active in the cause of abolition. She had always sympathized with slaves, and her friendship with Elizabeth Keckley had sharpened her awareness of their plight. Once she allowed a black Sunday school group to use the south lawn of the White House for a picnic. She also took up the cause of the so-called contrabands, thousands of Southern slaves who escaped to Union army camps. Together with Keckley, she raised money for clothes and blankets for the poverty-stricken **refugees**.

Emancipation

Lincoln was also pondering the situation of the slaves. Abolitionists urged him to free them all at once, but he feared alienating those slave states that had remained loyal to the Union: Kentucky, Missouri, Maryland, and Delaware. Finally he worked out a compromise plan. On September 22, 1862, a few days after the North had won a major victory at Antietam in Maryland, he announced the Emancipation Proclamation. It stated that as of January 1, 1863, slaves in any state in rebellion against the United States would be "then, thenceforward, and forever free." This effectively freed slaves in the Confederacy but not in the border states.

A commemorative print of the Emancipation Proclamation.

On January 1, 1863, Lincoln signed the proclamation. "If my name ever goes into history," Abraham said as he picked up the pen, "it will be for this act." Mary was very pleased. "It is a rich and precious legacy for my sons

33

Dead soldiers sprawl across the battlefield at Gettysburg, Pennsylvania. The Battle of Gettysburg was the bloodiest in the Civil War, with about 23,000 Union casualties and 28,000 Confederate casualties in all.

and one for which, I am sure, and believe, they will always bless God and their father," she said.

An Endless Conflict

Antietam did not, unfortunately, represent the turning point in the war that Lincoln was expecting. In the North, morale was at its lowest ebb during the winter and spring of 1863, as the Confederates piled up still more victories. Robert E. Lee had the most famous victory of his career at Chancellorsville, Virginia, on May 1–4. "My God! My God!" Lincoln moaned when he heard the news. "What will the country say?"

Lee decided to take the war to the North and pushed into Pennsylvania. There, on July 1–4, he met the Union army on the fields of Gettysburg—and lost. When General Grant had a major victory at Vicksburg the same day, Lincoln was cheered.

On November 19, Lincoln traveled to Gettysburg to give a speech at the dedication for the new Gettysburg National Cemetery. In it he reminded Americans why the war was being fought: to preserve a "government of the people, by the people, for the people." The **Gettysburg Address** summed up all of Lincoln's pride in, and hopes for, his nation.

By the spring of 1864, Grant and Lee were going at it head-to-head. In one month of fighting in Virginia—at Wilderness, Spotsylvania, and Cold Harbor—Grant lost 50,000 men; Lee lost 32,000. The fighting was so brutal that even Mary called Grant a "butcher." Lincoln, however, had faith in his general. "That man can fight," he would repeat.

To add to all his troubles, Lincoln was up for reelection, and it was by no means certain that he would win. Northerners were weary of the war and of the casualty lists posted in every newspaper. As summer moved into fall, Abraham waited impatiently for good news, haunting the War Department and reading the latest dispatches from the front. Mary fretted about her husband, who seemed so "broken-hearted, so completely worn out."

Mary had her own reasons for praying for reelection. The spending sprees in New York and Philadelphia had continued. By then, she was $27,000 in debt, an enormous sum in those days. If Abraham lost, merchants would demand immediate payment. "He will know all," she told Keckley. If he won, however, she could continue her extravagant spending a little longer. She might, she fooled herself, even pay back some of the money she owed.

The Gettysburg Address

Abraham Lincoln was not even the main speaker at the ceremony at Gettysburg National Cemetery. That honor went to Edward Everett, a famous orator who spoke for hours. Yet Everett himself recognized that Lincoln's address was brilliant. "I should be glad if I could flatter myself that I came as near to the central idea of the occasion in two hours as you did in two minutes," he wrote the president afterward. Today we recognize the Gettysburg Address as one of the most important speeches in American history:

Four score and seven years ago our fathers brought forth on this continent, a new nation, conceived in Liberty, and dedicated to the proposition that all men are created equal.

Now we are engaged in a great civil war, testing whether that nation, or any nation so conceived and so dedicated, can long endure. We are met on a great battle-field of that war. We have come to dedicate a portion of that field, as a final resting place for those who here gave their lives that that nation might live. It is altogether fitting and proper that we should do this.

But, in a larger sense, we can not dedicate—we can not consecrate—we can not hallow — this ground. The brave men, living and dead, who struggled here, have consecrated it, far above our poor power to add or detract. The world will little note, nor long remember what we say here, but it can never forget what they did here. It is for us the living, rather, to be dedicated here to the unfinished work which they who fought here have thus far so nobly advanced. It is rather for us to be here dedicated to the great task remaining before us—that from these honored dead we take increased devotion to that cause for which they gave the last full measure of devotion—that we here highly resolve that these dead shall not have died in vain—that this nation, under God, shall have a new birth of freedom—and that government of the people, by the people, for the people, shall not perish from the earth.

President Lincoln delivers his second inaugural address at the U.S. Capitol, March 4, 1865. He is in the center of the photograph, just above the small white table.

Peace at Last

Suddenly, the tide of war turned. On September 2, Union general William Tecumseh Sherman took the important Confederate city of Atlanta, Georgia. It was then not a matter of if, but when, the war would be won.

On November 8, 1864, Lincoln took the election with over 55 percent of the vote. Mary celebrated by going out and buying a $2,000 dress for the inauguration.

By the time Lincoln gave his second inaugural address on March 4, 1865, he was already looking forward to a postwar reconciliation between North and South. "With malice toward none, with charity for all; . . . let us strive on to finish the work we are in," he said. "To bind up the nation's wounds; . . . to do all which may achieve and cherish a just and lasting peace among ourselves, and with all nations."

The end finally came, not quickly but inevitably; on April 9, 1865, Confederate general Robert E. Lee of the Army of Northern Virginia surrendered to General Ulysses S. Grant of the Union army. Washington, D.C., went wild with joy. When thousands of people showed up to celebrate on the White House lawn, Lincoln asked the band to play the Southern rallying song "Dixie." It had always been one of his favorite tunes, he admitted, and now the Union could take it back. Tad waved a captured Confederate flag from a window, and the crowd cheered.

However, Abraham was still exhausted and not sleeping well. One night, he told his wife, he dreamed that he heard weeping. He explained that in his dream he wandered downstairs into the East Room. There he saw a corpse laid out in a coffin, surrounded by a crowd of mourning people. "Who is dead in the White House?" he asked a soldier. "The President," came the answer. "He was killed by an assassin!"

"That is horrid," Mary said. "I wish you had not told it."

"Well," Abraham said, "it is only a dream, Mary. Let us say no more about it, and try to forget it."

A Nightmare Comes True

Friday, April 14, dawned bright and cheerful, a lovely spring day. Late that afternoon, Abraham and Mary went out for their customary drive. They talked optimistically about the future and what they would do when Abraham left office. Perhaps they could travel to Europe or even to Jerusalem. Then they could return home to Springfield, and Lincoln could go back to being a country lawyer. The possibilities seemed endless.

That night they were going to Ford's Theater to see a light-hearted comedy called *Our American Cousin*. At the last moment, Mary had a headache, but Abraham persuaded her to come with him. He didn't want to go alone. When they arrived at Ford's Theater with their guests for the evening, Major Henry Rathbone and his fiancée, Clara Harris, the play had already started.

President Lincoln's decorated box at Ford's Theater, with his rocking chair on the right. When assassin John Wilkes Booth leaped from the box, his boot caught in the draped flag, and he fell to the stage and broke his shinbone.

37

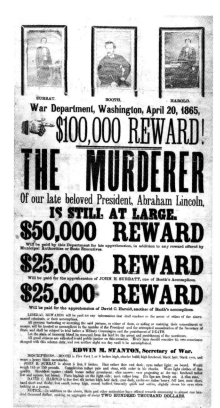

A broadside advertisement offers reward money for the capture of John Wilkes Booth and his co-conspirators. Booth spent fourteen days on the run. He was finally cornered and shot in a Virginia barn on April 26, 1865, and died a few hours later.

The group slipped into the private state box, decorated with festive patriotic bunting, as the orchestra played "Hail to the Chief." Abraham settled into the rocker set aside for him and took out his gold spectacles. During the third act, Mary drew close and took his hand. "What will Miss Harris think of my hanging on to you so?" she whispered. "She won't think anything about it," he replied.

They were his last words. A Southern actor named John Wilkes Booth slipped into the box behind them. Consumed by hatred for Lincoln, he was enraged by the defeat of the Confederacy and determined to avenge the loss. Taking careful aim, he pointed his derringer directly at the back of Lincoln's head. A shot rang out, and Lincoln slumped forward.

Booth jumped onto the stage, breaking his leg. With the cry, *Sic semper tyrannis!*" ("Thus always to tyrants!") he limped out the stage door. Mortally wounded, Lincoln was carried to a nearby house and laid diagonally across a too-small bed. When Mary reached him, she began kissing him frantically. "Do speak to me," she begged him. Then she fainted and had to be carried away.

Government officials, friends, and family crowded around the bed for a nine-hour death watch. Sobbing, Mary remained in the parlor, making occasional visits to the room. At dawn she came to

The last portrait taken of Abraham Lincoln, on April 10, 1865. His worn face reflects the strain of four years of brutal war.

President Lincoln's funeral procession marches up Pennsylvania Avenue in Washington, D.C. Lincoln's death caused the greatest outpouring of grief the nation had ever seen. Hundreds of thousands of people viewed his body and millions more paid their respects as the funeral train wound its way west to Springfield.

gaze on Abraham one last time. When she looked at his face, she realized it was almost over. "Oh, my God," she wailed. "And have I given my husband to die?"

At 7:22 A.M., April 15, 1865, Lincoln died. A few days later, Mary put on the black mourning clothes she would wear for the rest of her life. Abraham Lincoln was hers no longer. As Secretary of War Edwin Stanton said at the president's deathbed, "Now he belongs to the ages."

THE PRESIDENT'S WIDOW

On April 19, 1865, the day of his funeral, Abraham Lincoln's body lay in the East Room, just as he dreamed it would. Mary, though, remained upstairs, too frantic with grief to attend. Afterward, as the train bearing her husband's coffin chugged slowly back to Springfield, she stayed secluded, seeing only Elizabeth Keckley and Tad. She was so hysterical that Tad threw his arms around her and burst out, "Don't cry so, Mama, or you will make me cry too! You will break my heart!"

After five weeks, Mary and Tad moved to Chicago, where her oldest son, Robert, was a lawyer. Still in debt and haunted by fears of bankruptcy, she tried to sell her clothes, but when the newspapers heard of the sale, they attacked her, calling her "vulgar" and "greedy." Humiliated, Mary escaped to Europe. There she lived in spas while Tad attended a boarding school. Although her legacy from her husband had made her by most measures a wealthy woman, she tried hard to get a pension from Congress. Eventually it awarded her $3,000 a year, not as much as she had asked for but sufficient to live on.

Mary Lincoln's wardrobe, on exhibition in New York City, October 26, 1867. Mary's attempt to raise money by selling some of her clothes turned into a public relations fiasco.

In May 1871, she returned with Tad to America. Unfortunately, Tad caught a cold on the ocean liner. This cold turned into a bad chest infection, and on July 13, Tad died after being nursed by his mother. Again, Mary was abandoned. "I feel there is no life for me, without my idolized Taddie," she said. "One by one, I have consigned to their resting place my idolized ones, and now, in this world, there is nothing left for me, but the deepest anguish and desolation."

The Threat of Insanity

Then began a period of wandering from spa to spa and hotel to hotel. Mary attended séances, or supposed meetings with spirits, in which spiritualists promised her contact with her dead family. She even visited a "spirit photographer," who photographed the shadow of Abraham Lincoln standing behind her, his hands on her shoulders. Mary became more and more eccentric. She shopped for things she could not possibly use: a dozen pairs of lace curtains at once for a home she didn't have, or ten pairs of gloves. Her rooms were packed with goods and trunks that she never opened. She was so nervous that she often requested the chambermaid sleep in the same room with her. She was also taking large doses of chloral hydrate, a medication to help her sleep.

Mary was miserable, eccentric, and possibly confused by drugs, but she was not crazy. Nonetheless, Robert, increasingly embarrassed by his mother's behavior and worried about her extravagant spending, signed the papers to have her committed to a hospital for the insane. In court, Mary sat in silence and dignity as doctors, salespeople, and hotel employees attested to her erratic behavior. "Oh, Robert, to think that my son would do this to me," was all she said to him. The all-male jury pronounced Mary insane, and she was dispatched to a sanitarium, at that time a polite name for a mental hospital.

Determined to fight for her freedom, Mary was the model inmate. She contacted her friend, lawyer Myra Bradwell, the first female lawyer in Illinois. Bradwell, declaring that Mary was "no more insane than I am," won Mary her freedom in just three months and three weeks. Mary retreated to her sister Elizabeth's home in Springfield to recover. However, the damage was done. Mary would never forgive her eldest, now her only, son for betraying her. For his part, Robert would never believe his mother wholly sane.

Mary knew her reputation had been damaged permanently. "My former friends will never cease to regard me as a lunatic," she told Elizabeth. "I feel it in their soothing manner. If I should say

Robert Todd Lincoln in the 1870s. As the only surviving Lincoln son, Robert had a very difficult time dealing with his distraught mother in the last decade of her life.

the moon is made of green cheese, they would heartily and smilingly agree with me."

Final Rest

Again, Mary set off on a meandering tour of Europe. Though she was only fifty-eight years old, her suffering had made her old and ill. Six years later, she went back to Springfield for the last time. There, in the same house in which she and Abraham Lincoln had been married forty years before, she died on July 16, 1882.

At her funeral, the pastor compared the Lincolns to two pine trees that had grown so close together that when one was struck by lightning, the other suffered. "They had virtually both been killed at the same time," the pastor said. "So it seems to me today, that we are only looking at death placing its seal upon the lingering victim of a past calamity."

Mary was buried beside Abraham, Eddie, Willie, and Tad Lincoln in Oak Ridge Cemetery in Springfield. Finally, she had her family around her once again.

Robert Todd Lincoln

The eldest son of Abraham and Mary Todd Lincoln witnessed the deaths of three brothers, the assassination of his father, and the mental disintegration of his mother. Yet Robert Todd Lincoln still managed to have a useful, distinguished career. He was appointed to General Ulysses S. Grant's staff in the last days of the Civil War and was in Washington, D.C., when Lincoln was shot. After keeping vigil at the bedside of his dying father, Robert was chief mourner at the funeral. Afterward, he became a lawyer and businessman in Chicago. Robert served as secretary of war for President James A. Garfield in 1881–85 and ambassador to England for President Benjamin Harrison in 1889–92. Strangely, he was in the vicinity when both Presidents Garfield and William McKinley were assassinated, in 1881 and 1901, respectively. Robert recognized uneasily a "certain fatality about the presidential function when I am present."

Robert married and had three children. The last descendant of Mary Todd and Abraham Lincoln died in 1985.

1809	Abraham Lincoln born February 12
1818	Mary Todd born December 13
1831	Abraham Lincoln moves to New Salem, Illinois
1834	Abraham Lincoln elected to Illinois state legislature
1837	Abraham Lincoln moves to Springfield, Illinois
1839	Mary Todd moves to Springfield, Illinois; meets Abraham Lincoln
1842	Mary Todd and Abraham Lincoln marry November 4
1843	Robert Todd Lincoln born August 1
1846	Edward (Eddie) Baker Lincoln born March 10; Abraham Lincoln elected to U.S. House of Representatives
1850	Eddy Lincoln dies; William (Willy) Wallace Lincoln born December 21
1853	Thomas (Tad) Lincoln born April 4
1854	Kansas-Nebraska Act passed by Congress
1858	Abraham Lincoln loses race for U.S. Senate
1860	Abraham Lincoln elected president; South Carolina secedes from the Union
1861	Abraham Lincoln inaugurated; Confederates fire on Fort Sumter in South Carolina; Civil War begins
1862	Willy Lincoln dies February 20; Union wins battle of Shiloh, April 6–7; Union takes New Orleans April 25; Union wins battle of Antietam September 17
1863	Abraham Lincoln signs Emancipation Proclamation January 1; Confederacy wins Battle of Chancellorsville May 1–4; Union wins Battle of Gettysburg July 1–4; Lincoln delivers Gettysburg Address November 19
1864	Generals Robert E. Lee and Ulysses S. Grant fight the battles of the Wilderness, Spotsylvania, and Cold Harbor May 5–June 3; Union occupies Atlanta, Georgia, September 2; Abraham Lincoln is reelected November 8
1865	Robert E. Lee surrenders to Ulysses S. Grant April 9; Abraham Lincoln dies April 15
1871	Tad Lincoln dies July 13
1875	Mary Lincoln declared "insane" and confined to mental hospital, then later freed
1882	Mary Todd Lincoln dies July 16

GLOSSARY

abolitionist—person who wants to outlaw or end slavery.

assassination—murder of a public figure by a sudden, surprise attack.

barracks—buildings that house soldiers.

casualty—soldier who is killed, wounded, or missing.

Confederate States of America—name of the nation formed by the eleven states that seceded from the United States in 1860 and 1861.

Congress—branch of the United States government in charge of legislation and taxation and which is composed of the Senate and the House of Representatives.

contraband—today, smuggled goods or goods that are forbidden to own or trade. During the time of the Civil War, property rightfully seized in wartime.

corset—rectangular strip of cloth that is stiffened with bones and wraps around a woman's midriff. It is pulled tight with laces and hooks to make the waist smaller.

democracy—system of government run by the people themselves, often through a system of representatives.

emancipate—to set free from the control of others, usually referring to slaves.

Emancipation Proclamation (1863)—President Lincoln's declaration freeing the slaves in the Confederate states.

Gettysburg Address (1863)—speech given by President Lincoln at the dedication of the cemetery established after the Battle of Gettysburg.

House of Representatives—lower house of the United States Congress. The number of congressional representatives from each state changes according to population.

inaugural address—speech given by a new president when he is sworn into office.

inauguration—ceremonial swearing in of a person into office, often referring to the swearing in of a new president.

latitude—distance north or south of the equator, measured by degrees.

legislator—member of the branch of government that makes laws.

militia—army of citizens who serve as soldiers during an emergency.

milldam—dam built to create a pond. The pond's waters power a mill's wheel.

refugee—person who flees to another land to escape danger or harassment.

renominate—to propose a candidate for relection to office.

running mate—candidate running for a lower office than the main candidate, usually referring to a vice president.

secede—to withdraw from or leave an organization, in this case referring to the United States.

senator—member of the upper house of the United States Congress. Each state is represented by two senators.

tuberculosis—contagious disease that attacks mainly the lungs.

typhoid fever—contagious disease that is often marked by fevers and headaches.

Union—during the Civil War, the states that did not secede from the United States of America.

Whig Party—American political party formed in 1834, especially supportive of business and commerce. After the party fell apart, most Whigs joined the newly formed Republican Party.

FURTHER INFORMATION

Further Reading

Chang, Ina. *A Separate Battle: Women in the Civil War*. New York: Puffin, 1996.

Collins, David R. *Shattered Dreams: The Story of Mary Todd Lincoln* (Notable Americans). Greensboro, NC: Morgan Reynolds, 1994.

Ford, Carin T. *The Battle of Gettysburg and Lincoln's Gettysburg Address* (Civil War Library). Berkeley Heights, NJ: Enslow Publishers, 2004.

Gormley, Beatrice. *First Ladies: Women Who Called the White House Home*. Madison, WI: Turtleback Books, 2004.

Hakim, Joy. *War, Terrible War* (A History of US). New York: Oxford University Press, 2002.

Heinrichs, Ann. *The Emancipation Proclamation* (We the People). Minneapolis: Compass Point Books, 2002.

January, Brendan. *The Lincoln-Douglas Debates*. New York: Children's Press, 1998.

Marrin, Albert. *Commander in Chief: Abraham Lincoln and the Civil War*. New York: Dutton Children's Books, 2002.

Mayo, Edith P. (ed.) *The Smithsonian Book of the First Ladies: Their Lives, Times, and Issues*. New York: Henry Holt/ Smithsonian Institution, 1996.

McPherson, James M. *Fields of Fury: The American Civil War*. New York: Atheneum, 2002.

Otfinoski, Steven. *John Wilkes Booth and the Civil War* (Notorious Americans and Their Times). Woodbridge, CT: Blackbirch Marketing, 1998.

Santow, Dan. *Mary Todd Lincoln 1818–1882* (Encyclopedia of First Ladies). New York: Children's Press, 1999.

Sullivan, George. *In Their Own Words: Abraham Lincoln*. New York: Scholastic Reference, 2001.

Symonds, Craig L. *American Heritage History of the Battle of Gettysburg*. New York: HarperCollins Publishers Inc., 2004.

Places to visit:

Abraham Lincoln Birthplace National Historic Site
2995 Lincoln Farm Road
Hodgenville, KY 42748
(270) 358-3137

Ford's Theatre National Historic Site
511 10th Street, N.W.
Washington, D.C. 20004
(202) 426-6924

Gettysburg National Military Park
97 Taneytown Road
Gettysburg, PA 17325-2804
(717) 334-1124

FURTHER INFORMATION

Lincoln Boyhood National Memorial
Indiana Highway 162
Lincoln City, IN 47552
(812) 937-4541

Lincoln Home National Historic Site
413 South Eighth Street
Springfield, IL 62701-1905
(217) 492-4241 ext. 221

Lincoln Memorial
900 Ohio Drive, S.W.
Washington, D.C. 20024
(202) 426-6841

Mary Todd Lincoln House
578 West Main Street
Lexington, KY 40507
(859) 233-9999

National Archives
700 Pennsylvania Avenue., N.W.
Washington, D.C. 20408
(866) 325-7208

The National First Ladies' Library
Education and Research Center
205 Market Avenue South
Canton, OH 44702
(330) 452-0876

Smithsonian National Museum of
American History
14th Street and Constitution Ave. N.W.
Washington, D.C. 20013
(202) 633-1000

White House
1600 Pennsylvania Avenue, N.W.
Washington, D.C. 20500

(202) 456-2121

United States Capitol
Constitution Avenue
Washington, D.C. 20515
(202) 224-3121

Web sites

Abraham Lincoln Research Site

members.aol.com/RVSNorton/Lincoln2.html

Ford's Theater National Historic Site

www.nps.gov/foth

Gettysburg National Military Park

www.nps.gov/gett/

Lincoln Boyhood National Memorial
Lincoln City, Indiana

www.nps.gov/libo

Lincoln Home National Historic Site
Springfield, Illinois

www.nps.gov/liho

The National First Ladies Library

www.firstladies.org

The White House

www.whitehouse.gov

INDEX

Page numbers in *italics* indicate maps and diagrams. Page numbers in **bold** indicate other illustrations

About the Author

Ruth Ashby has written many award-winning biographies and nonfiction books for children, including *Herstory*, *The Elizabethan Age*, and *Pteranodon: The Life Story of a Pterosaur*. She lives on Long Island with her husband, daughter, and dog, Nubby.